Dominic Wood's

MAGIC
Book

RED FOX

This book I dedicate to my grandmother, who we all miss, but still love! This one's for you, Granny. Hope you're OK. x

A note to Sandi. I love you with all my heart, sweetpea! You give me strength, love and security. You really are my Debbi McGee. Ha! 'Now that's magic!' x

DOMINIC WOOD'S MAGIC BOOK

A RED FOX BOOK 0 09 944767 3

First published in Great Britain by The Bodley Head,
an imprint of Random House Children's Books

Bodley Head edition published 2002
Red Fox edition published 2003

1 3 5 7 9 10 8 6 4 2

Text © Dominic Wood, 2002

With thanks to Mark Leveridge, photographer Roddy Paine and models, Cornelia, François and Pascal Colman, Becky and Josie Paine, Reece Woodhams and Kelly-Ann Yeung.

The right of Dominic Wood to be identified as the author of this work
has been asserted in accordance with the Copyright, Designs and Patents Act 1988.

Red Fox Books are published by Random House Children's Books,
61–63 Uxbridge Road, London W5 5SA,
a division of The Random House Group Ltd,
in Australia by Random House Australia (Pty) Ltd,
20 Alfred Street, Milsons Point, Sydney, NSW 2061, Australia,
in New Zealand by Random House New Zealand Ltd,
18 Poland Road, Glenfield, Auckland 10, New Zealand,
and in South Africa by Random House (Pty) Ltd,
Endulini, 5A Jubilee Road, Parktown 2193, South Africa

THE RANDOM HOUSE GROUP Limited Reg. No. 954009
www.kidsatrandomhouse.co.uk
www.dominicwood.co.uk

A CIP catalogue record for this book is available from the British Library.
Printed in Singapore

Check out the star rating to see how difficult the trick is to learn or perform:

 easy

★☆☆☆☆ easy

★★☆☆☆ moderate

★★★☆☆ difficult

★★★★☆ very difficult

★★★★★ extremely difficult

You can master all the tricks in this book with practice!

CONTENTS

INTRODUCTION

Well, well, well. Here we are again! My second magic book for you guys and the tricks are even better and more amazing than before.

Hopefully by now you will have read my other book, *Simply Magic*, and practised, perfected and performed all the cool tricks! I'm sure your audiences have been screaming out for more, and guess what … you can give them more! More floating, more vanishing, more mind-reading – a whole lot more magic!

Don't worry if you haven't read *Simply Magic* – all the tricks in this book are easy to learn with my step-by-step instructions.

None of the tricks here uses expensive props or takes years to perfect. Every trick uses bits and bobs and odds and ends from around the house, from Tic Tacs to rubber bands.

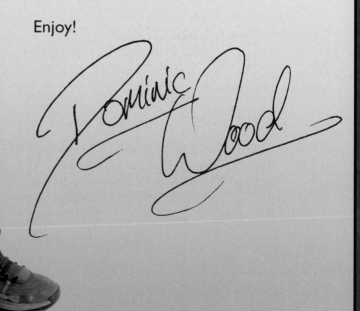

My personal favourites in this book are 'Egyptian Cups' and 'Floating Fruit'. I really recommend you try them. I've done all these tricks on CBBC and other TV shows, and they amaze the audience every time!

So, if you want to be a wizard magician, just turn the page and off you go!

Enjoy!

Dominic Wood

TOP TIPS

With all the great tricks in this book you'll be able to put on a spectacular show to entertain your family and friends. To ensure your performance goes with a bang, follow these top tips . . .

1 Make a list of the tricks you want to put in your show – around six is probably enough. Two short shows are better than one endless one!

2 Make sure you have collected together everything you need in advance. Nothing is worse than having to stop halfway through a trick to fetch something. It's a good idea to have a box where you can keep all your props.

3 Try to choose tricks that can be seen by the whole audience. If you are doing a show for a small number of people, select tricks with small objects. If you have a larger audience, choose tricks with bigger items.

4 Try to be imaginative when you are performing. It is better to make up something magical about a trick than simply to describe what you are doing.

5 When doing your tricks, remember to look at your audience and speak loudly and clearly. And don't forget to smile! Doing magic can sometimes make you nervous, but try to relax and enjoy it!

MINDFUL MAGIC

Being a good magician means getting organized! A prop box is a great way of keeping all your tricks together and ensuring no one discovers your secrets!

WHAT YOU NEED
- A shoe box
- Wrapping paper
- A pen
- Scissors
- Sticky tape
- A stapler
- A shoelace

2 Remove the lid and cut the wrapping paper to size, leaving twice the width of the lid's rim around the rectangle. Fold each edge of the paper up to the pen line. Then fold in again along the line.

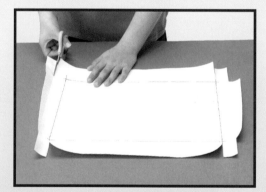

3 Unfold the paper and cut out a small rectangle at each corner along the outside corner creases and then a line along the inner crease up to the pen marks. You should be left with two edges with tabs and two edges without.

1 Place the lid of the shoe box on top of the wrapping paper, both face down, and draw around the lid to make a rectangle.

★ STAR TIPS ★

Always be extra careful when cutting and sticking. Put newspaper down in case of spillages and ask an adult if you need help.

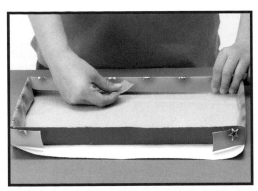

4 Place the shoe-box lid face down again so it lines up with the rectangle. Fold the tabbed edges around the rim and secure them with sticky tape. Do the same with the remaining two edges. The corners will be nice and neat.

5 Repeat steps 1–4 with the box.

6 You may want to attach the lid so that no one can see inside. Stick some pieces of tape along the inside of one long edge of the lid and attach them to the outside of the corresponding edge of the box. Staple one end of the shoelace to the inside top edge of the lid and the other end to the inside corresponding edge of the box.

CREATIVE PATTER

The best magicians are the ones who engage their audience with jokes, good stories or a whole lot of mystery. Try some of these openers to get people in the mood:

You may not think this to look at me but I am truly telepathic . . .

I always win the toss at the start of matches – watch!

I'm such a card sharp, I have to be careful not to cut myself!

People say I have an electric personality – let me show you why.

Getting the wrong flavour sweet never bothers me – I just use my magic to get what I want.

JUMPING BAND

A rubber band magically jumps between your fingers!

PERFORMANCE

1 Show the rubber band and slip it over the first two fingers of your right hand. Ask the audience to note where the band is.

3 With the back of your closed fist facing the audience, quickly open your hand. The band will shoot off the first two fingers and end up hanging round the third and fourth fingers!

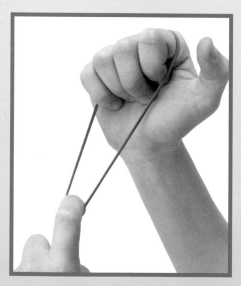

2 With your left hand pull the band down over your right palm. Close your hand so that all four fingers go inside the band and release it so it runs along the backs of your fingers.

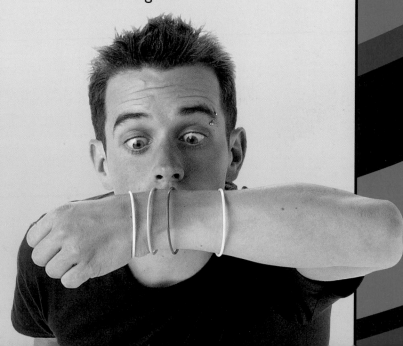

NUMBER FUN

Random numbers are selected from a grid by three members of the audience. When the sums are done, the remaining figures add up to your prediction!

WHAT YOU NEED
- A pad of paper
- A pen

PREPARATION

1 Write the number 34 on a piece of paper and fold the paper in half so the number is hidden. This is your prediction.

2 Draw a four-by-four grid on the pad and write the numbers 1 to 16 in the squares.

★ STAR TIPS ★
You could ask a member of the audience to add up the numbers for you.

PERFORMANCE

1 Draw attention to the piece of paper with your hidden prediction and place it in view.

2 Show the grid and ask a member of the audience to choose a number. Put a circle round this number and cross out all the others in the same row and column. Repeat this with two more audience members until one number is left untouched, then circle that.

3 Add the four circled numbers together and they will always make 34. Reveal your prediction and your audience will be amazed!

Money Magic

A coin is marked with a sticker and hidden among five others while your back is turned. Using your magic powers you can instantly identify the marked coin!

WHAT YOU NEED
• Six 2p coins
• A small white label
• A pen

PREPARATION

1 Two-pence pieces of varied ages have different pictures of the queen on them – it is her crown that differs the most. Find five two-pence pieces with the same picture and one two-pence piece with a different picture.

2 Stack the coins with their heads facing down, making sure the 'odd' coin is on the top.

PERFORMANCE

1 Attach the label to the tail side of the top, 'odd' coin and ask a member of the audience to initial it.

2 Turn over the coins so they are tails down and spread them out in a row.

3 Ask your helper to mix up the
coins while your back is turned
so that the marked coin is lost
among the others.

4 Turn round and remove the coins
one by one, leaving the 'odd' coin
until last. When your helper turns
it over they will be surprised to
find it is their initialled coin.

 ★★☆☆☆

Bangle Wizard

A circle of cord and a bangle are dropped separately into a paper bag. When removed they are mysteriously joined together!

PREPARATION

1. Cut along the three edges of one of the bags and discard one side so you are left with a piece of paper exactly the same size as the other bag. Slip this inside the complete bag so you have one bag with two compartments.

2. Hang a bangle on one length of cord and tie the ends of the cord together.

3. Place this into one of the compartments in the bag.

PERFORMANCE

1. Show your audience the other cord and tie the ends together.

2. Pick up the bag and hold the top open so that the empty compartment shows. It will look as if the bag is empty.

3. Drop the circle of cord into the empty compartment of the bag and then drop the bangle in as well.

4. Snap your fingers over the bag, reach into the other compartment and pull out the cord attached to the bangle.

Piercing Pencil

A pencil wrapped in a hanky magically moves from one side to the other.

WHAT YOU NEED
- A plain handkerchief
- A pencil

PERFORMANCE

3 Grip the pencil through the hanky and roll it up loosely towards the top edge with the pencil still inside.

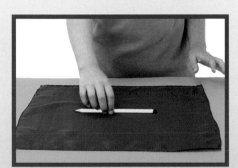

1 Open out the handkerchief and lay it flat on a table. Place the pencil lengthways in the centre of the hanky.

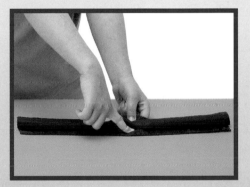

4 When you reach the top, the edge underneath will pop out. Take this edge and pull it towards you so the hanky unrolls. The pencil will now be under the hanky!

2 Take hold of the two bottom corners of the hanky and fold it in half, over the pencil. Make sure the bottom edge overlaps the top edge.

★★☆☆☆

Mind Reader

Using your mysterious mind-reading techniques you are able to tell a member of the audience the word they are thinking of from a book!

WHAT YOU NEED

- Two identical hardback books with removable jackets
- One hardback book of the same size with a removable jacket

PREPARATION

1 Remove the jacket from one of the two identical books and replace it with the jacket of the third, non-identical one. You now have two books that look different but are actually the same book!

PERFORMANCE

1 Show the two supposedly different books and hand the one with its original jacket to a member of the audience.

2 Ask another member of the audience to call 'stop' as you riffle through the pages of the other, 'false' book. When they do, stop riffling, hold the book towards them and ask them to call out one of the two page numbers shown.

3 Look at the page as if you are checking the page number and secretly look at the first word on that page, then put the book away.

4 Ask your first helper to open their book at the same page as was called out. Tell them to find the first word on that page and to repeat it in their head.

5 Pretend that you are reading their mind and call out the word you saw in the other book. They will be amazed that you can read their mind!

HEY PRESTO!

★ **STAR TIPS** ★

Try to find books without the title written at the top of each page to make certain you don't get caught out. You can look as if you're really concentrating and struggling to read your helper's mind!

★★☆☆☆

Penny Pincher

A coin vanishes from underneath a handkerchief.

WHAT YOU NEED
- A 10p piece
- A handkerchief

PERFORMANCE

1 Shake out the handkerchief with your right hand and place it over your left fist.

2 In your right hand, pick up the ten-pence piece and take it under the handkerchief. As soon as it is out of sight, drop the coin into your left sleeve.

 ★ STAR TIPS ★
Remember to keep your left arm bent a little when you take your fist from under the handkerchief or else the coin may fall out of your sleeve!

3 Keep your right hand under the handkerchief and bring out your left hand. Show your audience that this hand is empty and use it to pick up the handkerchief in the middle as if you were holding the coin through the handkerchief.

4 Remove your right hand and show it to be empty. Snap your fingers over the handkerchief and shake it out so the audience can see that the coin has vanished!

Super Saucer

A cup is magically balanced on the thin edge of a saucer!

PERFORMANCE

1 Take the saucer in your left hand and hold it steady with your right hand.

3 Seen from the front, it looks as if the cup is balancing all on its own on the thin edge of the saucer!

2 With your left hand pick up the cup and carefully balance it on the top edge of the saucer. As you do so, secretly extend your right thumb up and under the cup so the cup can rest on your thumb for extra support.

★ STAR TIPS ★

This is a great stunt to do at the dinner table but make sure no one is sitting at your side or behind you. Practise this trick over a soft surface to make sure you don't break any crockery!

PAUL FRANK

TIC TAC SWITCH

A coloured Tic Tac mysteriously changes into a white Tic Tac in front of your audience's eyes!

WHAT YOU NEED
- A box of white Tic Tacs
- A box of coloured Tic Tacs

PREPARATION

1 Remove one white Tic Tac and discard the box.

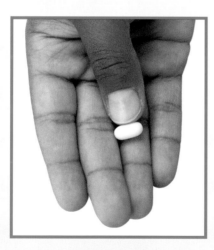

2 Hold the Tic Tac in your right hand between your thumb and halfway down your middle fingers.

PERFORMANCE

1 Pick up the coloured box of Tic Tacs and place it in your right hand on top of the concealed white Tic Tac.

2 Open the flap with your left hand and shake the container so that a coloured Tic Tac falls into your left palm. Offer it to a member of the audience and repeat this once or twice.

3 Say that you prefer the traditional white Tic Tacs to the coloured ones, then secretly cover the opening of the box with your thumb.

4 Shake the container over your left hand again and allow the white Tic Tac concealed in your right hand to drop into your left palm.

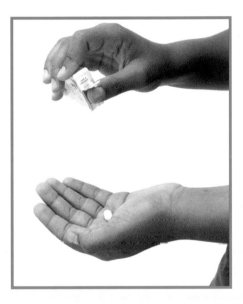

5 Hold your left hand out to the audience to show that the Tic Tac has changed colour!

★ **STAR TIPS** ★

When you tip the coloured Tic Tacs out, try holding your thumb slightly over the hole so that only one Tic Tac falls out at a time. This means the way you are holding the container will remain the same.

★★★☆☆

DICE BOX

When a dice is shaken inside a matchbox you are able to predict what number comes up.

PREPARATION

WHAT YOU NEED
- Two empty matchboxes
- Two small identical dice
- Glue
- Scissors
- Sticky tape
- A pen
- Paper

① Carefully cut off the end of one of the matchbox drawers. Using the sticky tape, stick the cut-out piece in the middle of the second matchbox drawer to create a partition.

② Put some glue on the side of one of the dice that shows the number 3. Stick it into the bottom right-hand corner of the divided drawer, so it is showing the number 4, then slip the drawer into its cover.

PERFORMANCE

① Hold the matchbox in front of you with the secured dice on your right. Push the matchbox open to the left so that the empty half of the drawer is seen. Do not open it too far or you will reveal the partition in the middle.

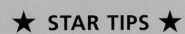
2 Drop the loose dice inside and shut the box. Shake it a little, then tilt the box down towards the top left corner and push the drawer open to show the number. Shut the box and repeat a couple more times.

3 Give the closed box to a spectator and ask them to shake it and put it down. Write the number 4 on the piece of paper. Do not show it but fold it up and put it to one side.

4 Pick up the box and turn it so that the secured dice is on the left. Tilt the box down towards the top left corner and push it open to reveal the secured dice. Show your prediction with a flourish!

★★★☆☆

Coloured Coins

A member of the audience is given a coin marked blue and a coin marked red. The blue coin is removed from the spectator's fist but when they open their hand they are still holding the blue coin and you now have the red coin. Spooky!

WHAT YOU NEED
• Three 10p coins
• Three small red stickers
• Three small blue stickers

PREPARATION

1 Stick a blue sticker on both sides of one coin, a red sticker on both sides of another coin and a red sticker on one side and a blue sticker on the other side of the last coin.

2 Place the red-blue coin with the red side facing upwards on a table, next to the all-blue coin. Put the all-red coin in your right pocket.

PERFORMANCE

1 Show the two coins and explain that you have put stickers on them so that you can tell one from the other.

2 Casually pick up the all-blue coin and show both sides before placing it on top of the red-blue coin.

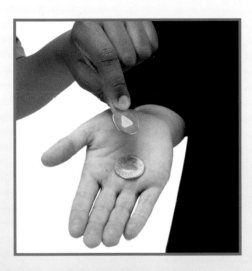

3 Ask a member of the audience to hold out their right hand, then pick up the two coins and place them on the middle of their palm. Spread the coins out so they can see the 'red' coin under the blue one and then square them up again.

4 Ask your helper to close their fingers over the coins and turn their hand over, telling them to hold the coins loosely.

5 Use your right finger and thumb to reach into their fist and slide out the top coin. You will be holding the red-blue coin with its blue side facing up so it will appear to be the blue coin. Tell the audience that you have removed the blue coin.

6 Openly put the red-blue coin in your right pocket. Say that, as you have the blue coin, the helper must have the red one, but that you are going to make the coins change places. When the helper opens their hand, they will be surprised to find that they are holding the blue coin. At that moment, bring the all-red coin out of your pocket to be examined.

Perfect Prediction

A member of the audience selects a playing card which magically matches your secret prediction.

PREPARATION

WHAT YOU NEED
- A small stack of playing cards
- A piece of paper
- An envelope
- A pen

1 Choose a card from the stack to be your prediction, write down its value on the piece of paper and seal it in the envelope.

2 Place your chosen card at the bottom of the pile.

PERFORMANCE

1 Show the audience the envelope containing your prediction and leave it in view.

2 Pick up the cards and spread them out face down. Then square the cards into a neat pile in your left hand, making sure that the left end of the stack is covered by your hand.

3 Bring your right hand to the visible end of the pile and with your middle finger secretly push back your chosen card at the bottom so that it is set back a little further than the rest of the stack.

4 Say that you are going to go through the pack until a member of the audience shouts 'stop' and, using the middle finger of your right hand, slide the second to bottom card out from under the pile and place it on top of the stack. Repeat this until an audience member shouts 'stop'. You may have to remind them to do so!

5 Square up the cards and turn them over to show your chosen card, which has remained on the bottom of the stack the whole time.

6 Ask another member of the audience to open the envelope and read out your prediction. They are sure to be amazed!

★★★☆☆

Marble Marvel

Six different-coloured marbles are removed from a bag but not shown to anyone. Using your marvellous magic, you are able to predict the colour of the last marble left in the bag.

WHAT YOU NEED
- Seven different-coloured marbles
- A square, cloth bag

PREPARATION

1 Put all the marbles in the bag except, for example, a blue one.

2 Conceal the blue marble in your right hand and grip the top right corner of the bag.

PERFORMANCE

1 Explain that there are six different-coloured marbles in the bag and that you are going to ask five members of the audience to take out one marble each without looking at it or showing it to anyone.

2 As you offer the bag to each audience member, keep hold of the top right corner with your right hand and grip the top left corner with your left hand.

3 When five marbles have been removed, let go of the left corner with your left hand so the last marble rolls into the bottom left corner. Then re-grip the bag here so you are holding the marble through the bag.

4 Tilt the bag slightly to the right and secretly drop the blue marble still concealed in your right hand into the bag.

5 Tell the audience that you believe all the marbles have been removed except the blue one and ask your helpers to check the colours of their marbles.

6 Move your right hand to the top left corner, keeping your left hand holding the marble at the bottom. Ask a member of the audience to hold out their hands and tip the bag so the blue marble falls out into their hands.

★ **STAR TIPS** ★
You can make this more dramatic by asking the audience members to call out the colour of their marbles when they check them.

WOW!

SECRET VISION

A card is chosen from a pack and slipped inside a little envelope. Using your secret vision, you are able to see the card through the envelope!

WHAT YOU NEED
- A small, brown pay envelope
- A pair of nail scissors
- A pack of cards

PREPARATION

1 Turn the envelope over so the address side is facing towards you and the flap is at the top.

2 Take the nail scissors and cut a small hole out of the bottom right corner of the envelope. The hole must be big enough to show the card number and suit when it is slipped into the envelope.

PERFORMANCE

1 Spread out the pack of cards face down and ask a member of the audience to pick one. Tell them to look at the card but to make sure you don't see it.

2 Take hold of the envelope and put it down so that the side with the hole is underneath. Slide the card face down into the envelope and close the flap but do not seal it.

3 Pick up the envelope in your left hand at the bottom left corner, thumb on top, fingers underneath, so that your fingers cover the hole, and raise the envelope so that the side with the cutout is facing the audience.

4 Turn the envelope over by twisting your left hand so that the flap tilts towards you and then down towards the ground. In one movement, take the envelope in your right hand and let go with your left.

5 The address side will now be facing you with the cutout at the top left. Look at the card value but try not to make it obvious!

6 Place the envelope on a table with the cutout underneath and call out the value of the card. Slide it out and turn it over for everyone to see.

★ STAR TIP ★

You can build up the tension of this trick by emphasizing your magic powers. Tell your audience that it is only possible to see through the envelope with your amazing secret vision. Then stare at the envelope for a few moments – just like Superman – before you reveal the card value!

Static Match

A match is charged with static electricity so that it makes another match jump back in shock!

PERFORMANCE

1 Take one of the matches and rub it on either your own or an audience member's sleeve, saying that you are charging it with static electricity.

2 Take the second match and lay it in the centre of your left palm with the head facing right.

3 Hold the 'charged-up' match in your right hand between thumb and forefinger and rest the nail of your third finger on the very end of the match.

4 Bring the head of the 'charged-up' match just in front of the head of the match in your left hand. The moment the match heads touch, pull the third fingernail of your right hand towards you so that the nail clicks off the end of the match.

5 The 'charged-up' match will jump slightly, knocking against the match in your left palm and making it look as if it has jumped back in shock!

★ STAR TIP ★
This trick may need a lot of practice but when you've got the knack it will look very effective. Sometimes, if you catch it just right, the loose match may shoot off your hand altogether!

Pencil Pruning

A normal pencil appears to shrink and then stretches back to its normal size.

PERFORMANCE

1 Hold the pencil to show its length, one end in each hand, and with any writing facing towards you. Slide both hands down the pencil until they nearly meet in the middle.

2 Grip the pencil in your left hand and rapidly stroke your right hand off the end. Bring it straight back to grip the right-hand side of the pencil again. Then quickly stroke the left hand off the other end.

WHAT YOU NEED
• A small pencil which fits comfortably inside your two fists

3 Repeat this several times as swiftly and as smoothly as possible and the pencil will look as if it has shrunk! Hold the pencil as in step 1 to finish.

★ STAR TIP ★
This trick is an optical illusion. It will look most effective if it is done quickly and slickly, so practise it well in front of a mirror first!

MONEY MAKER

A five-pound note appears between two postcards as if from thin air!

WHAT YOU NEED
- Four white postcards
- Glue
- A £5 note

PREPARATION

1 Cut out a small rectangle from the middle of one long edge of a postcard. Smear a very thin strip of glue around the remaining three edges and stick another postcard on top. This will leave a pocket with an opening down the side. Slide the five-pound note into the pocket, leaving some of it exposed in the opening.

2 Glue together the two remaining postcards so you are left with what looks like two identical, regular postcards.

PERFORMANCE

1 Hold the postcards level with the floor, with the 'pocket' postcard in your right hand and your fingers covering the cutout. Lift the cards up to show the underside and then back to face the floor.

3 Slide the top card to the right, secretly pulling out the five-pound note and place this card on top of the other one, trapping the five-pound note between the two cards. Snap your fingers and spread out the cards to reveal the note between them.

2 Place the left card on top of the 'pocket' card and take hold of them with both hands, resting the fingers of your right hand on the five-pound note.

★ **STAR TIPS** ★

You can really go to town describing this trick. Tell your audience you never have money troubles because you can make it appear from nowhere!

LOOPY LOOP

A knot is tied in a shoelace without the end of the lace going through the loop.

WHAT YOU NEED
• A shoelace

PERFORMANCE

1 Hold the shoelace up in both hands to show it to the audience.

2 With your right hand position the lace so a third of it hangs down over your left palm between your left thumb and index finger.

4 With your right hand, pick up the left end of the lace and, keeping your left hand still, pull it straight up. Allow the lace to slip between your left thumb and index finger, but make sure you catch back hold of the loop. The lace will end up threaded through the loop.

3 Use the right hand to wind the lace once round your left thumb, then bring the lace up to make a loop and grip it between the thumb and index finger of your left hand.

Floating Fruit

An orange is lifted from a table using only the tips of your fingers.

PREPARATION

1 Hide the cocktail stick in your right hand so it lies flat along your middle finger, with your thumb holding it in place.

PERFORMANCE

1 With your left hand place the orange on a table.

3 Holding the cocktail stick firmly against your straight fingers and thumb, slowly start to lift your right hand away from the table. The orange, stuck secretly on the cocktail stick, will be lifted off the table as if magically clinging to your fingertips!

2 Extend your right fingers out straight, making sure the cocktail stick remains hidden, and place them on top of the orange. In the same movement, use your right thumb to push the cocktail stick into the orange a little way.

★★★★★

EGYPTIAN CUPS

Three balls of tissue paper drop through the solid tops of two plastic cups.

PREPARATION

1. Roll each of the pieces of tissue paper into a small ball and put the three cups mouth up on a table.

2. Drop one ball into the first cup, then stack the second and third cups inside it. Drop the other three balls into the top cup.

PERFORMANCE

1. Tilt the stack of cups so that the three tissue balls roll out onto the table and place them in a row. In your left hand hold the stack of cups by their mouths and use your right hand to hold it underneath.

2. With your right hand pull out the bottom cup and turn it over quickly, so the secret ball is not seen, mouth down on the table. Repeat this action with the other two empty cups so they are in a row.

5 Repeat steps 3 and 4.

3 Pick up a tissue ball and place it on top of the right-hand cup. Stack the middle cup on top so the ball is trapped in between. Snap your fingers and lift the cups to reveal the new ball under the cups. It will look as if the ball has dropped through the right-hand cup.

6 Stack the middle cup on top of the right-hand cup and put the last ball on top of that, explaining that this ball has to pass through two cups. Finally, place the left-hand cup on top of the middle cup.

4 Turn the two cups mouth upwards and take them in your left hand. Pull out the bottom cup, which will have a new secret ball in it. Turn it over quickly and place it mouth down on the table, over the ball that has just been revealed. This will secretly add another ball under that cup. Put the other cup in your left hand back in the middle.

7 Snap your fingers and lift all three cups to reveal the three balls now underneath.

★ ★ ★ ★ ★

Head to Head

A perfectly normal coin becomes a two-headed coin and then changes back again!

WHAT YOU NEED
• A 50p or a 10p coin

PERFORMANCE

1 Show the coin to the audience and flip it between your hands to show it has two normal sides. Explain that you can make it two-headed and then change it back.

2 Place the coin, heads up, on your right fingers so that the edge is resting against the side of your third finger, which is raised up a little. Use your right thumb to steady the coin.

★ STAR TIP ★
This trick should be done smoothly and without a pause. Practise the move until you can do it really well before you attempt it in front of an audience.

3 Hold out your left hand, palm upwards. Bring your right hand over your left and turn it over so that the palm is facing the left hand. In the same movement, pull the coin with your right thumb so it turns over.

4 Release the coin so that it falls flat onto the left fingers. The coin will fall onto the left hand with the same side facing upwards as was shown at the start.

5 Repeat the trick as often as you like, showing just the heads side. Finally snap your fingers over the coin, and show both sides to your audience.

★ CREATIVE CLUE ★

There are plenty of ways to make the most of this trick. You can start by making a bet with a member of the audience, saying something like 'Heads I win, tails you lose!'

★★★★★

CUT THE CARD

A playing card is slipped into an envelope and cut in half with a pair of scissors. When the card is pulled out of the envelope it is magically restored in one piece!

WHAT YOU NEED
• A small, brown pay envelope
• A pair of scissors
• A sharp knife
• A playing card

PERFORMANCE

1 Hold up the envelope with the flap at the bottom and the cutout facing you. Firmly fold the envelope in half, bringing the flap towards you and saying this will help you make a clean cut. Make sure the point of the cut-out triangle is in line with the fold.

2 Place the envelope on a table with the flap facing towards the audience and the cutout face down. Slip the card inside, making sure the long edge of the card is pushed away from the side of the envelope with the cutout in it.

PREPARATION

1 Place the envelope on a hard surface with the address side up and the flap facing to the right. With the knife, carefully cut out a small triangle halfway along the top edge of the envelope, with the point of the triangle facing down. Make sure you only cut through one side of the envelope.

3 Pick up the envelope with your right hand, thumb on top, fingers underneath, so that your fingertips cover the cutout. Seal the envelope with your left hand.

4 Tilt up the envelope to show the audience the underside and keep turning it so the flap points towards you and then down towards the ground. In the same movement, grip the envelope by the bottom left corner with your left hand and release it with your right so the flap is now pointing down and the cutout is facing you on the right.

5 With your right hand, take the scissors and insert the blade nearest you inside the cutout and underneath the card inside. Cut across the fold in the envelope until you almost reach the other side. You will have cut through the side of the envelope facing the audience.

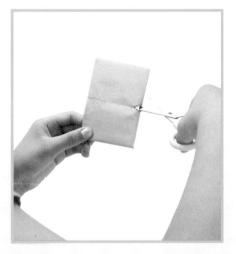

6 Carefully cut off the very top end of the envelope. Reach into the envelope and slowly slide the card out. Offer the card for inspection to a member of the audience, then quickly fold the envelope along the crease and pull the two halves sharply apart. Screw them up and discard.

★ **STAR TIP** ★

Making a soft fold halfway along the envelope before you cut out the triangle will help you find the middle. And if you score the crease with your fingernails when you are making the actual fold in front of your audience, the two halves will be easier to pull apart later.

★★★★★

Flying Coins

Three ten-pence pieces are placed down in a row. When the coins are covered with playing cards they jump from one card to another.

WHAT YOU NEED
- Two playing cards
- Four 10p coins
- A small piece of Blu-Tack

PREPARATION

1 Stick the Blu-Tack on the face of one of the cards just below the middle and press it down firmly.

2 Lightly stick one of the ten-pence pieces to the Blu-Tack so that it will stay attached when the card is lifted and put this 'sticky' card face down with the other card on top.

PERFORMANCE

1 Set out the three remaining ten-pence pieces in a row.

2 Pick up the cards and place them in your left hand. Using your left fingers, secretly release the coin under the 'sticky' card so that it falls into your palm. Be careful not to let anyone see this.

3 With your right hand, slide out the 'sticky' card and place it over the coin on the right. Make sure the Blu-Tack is over the coin and gently push on the back of the card so the coin sticks to the card.

4 With your right hand take the other card together with the secret coin from your left palm, and place them over the coin on the left. Make sure no one sees the secret coin as you do this.

SNAP!

5 With your right hand pick up the card on the right which now has a coin attached. Make sure no one can see this coin. Snap your fingers and lift up the card on the left to reveal the two coins underneath. Place the 'sticky' card in your left hand with the other card on top.

6 Secretly release the coin on the 'sticky' card, slide out the 'sticky' card and put it out of sight. Take the other card together with the coin from your left hand, keeping the coin hidden, and place them over the two coins already together on the table.

7 Pick up the visible coin and put it in your pocket. Explain that this coin will now have a long way to fly. Snap your fingers and lift up the remaining card to reveal all three coins together.

★ **STAR TIP** ★

Perform this trick on a soft surface such as a carpet or a table covered with a cloth. That way the cards won't look bumpy and the coins will make no noise when they are put down. Make sure the coins don't clink when placed together.

THE GREATEST MAGICIANS ON EARTH

When you perform the tricks in this book you are following in the footsteps of many great magicians who, for thousands of years, have been entertaining people with their clever ideas.

Nobody knows exactly when people started practising magic tricks but pictures have been discovered in Egyptian tombs of magicians performing the classic cups and balls trick (see page 36), and these drawings are more than 5,000 years old!

Early magicians tended to be priests who used simple magic tricks to inspire awe and wonder, but as time ran on magicians became associated with entertainment at fairs or other public gatherings, sometimes even in early theatres.

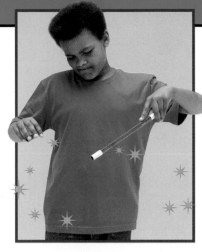

Unfortunately, during the Middle Ages, sleight-of-hand conjurors or jugglers, as they came to be known, were not always welcome. Many religious people saw in magicians a danger, and people who were accused of being witches were often killed, such was the fear they caused.

But in 1584, in the early days of printing, a book appeared called *The Discoverie of Witchcraft* in which the author, Reginald Scott, explained how magicians did their magic tricks. Today, this book is seen as the very first book on conjuring – a very early version of the book you hold in your hands right now!

From this time onwards magic and magicians gradually became more accepted, and by the nineteenth century, magic as an entertainment was becoming firmly established. There were a number of large travelling shows which toured the country presenting a full evening of stage magic at theatres and music halls, and this brought magic to the people. These magicians were often very theatrical and performed mind-reading tricks which stunned their audiences (see page 14).

By the twentieth century magicians were becoming increasingly well known. Harry Houdini, who started as a magician but became best known for his amazing escapes, was very popular and his name is still recognized today.

Most of the tricks described in this book are close-up tricks, which use small objects, and today this is the most popular form of magic. Television is now making worldwide superstars out of close-up magicians such as David Blaine, who takes his magic onto the streets. In many ways this is bringing magic back to where it began.

With the increasing popularity of cinemas and eventually the coming of television, the old theatres and music halls started to close down, unable to compete with the wonders of these new technologies. Many magicians simply adapted to this trend by changing the type of magic they performed. While some magicians such as David Copperfield still managed to tour the world with huge stage shows featuring ever more spectacular illusions, many, like Paul Daniels, took to the small screen and most magicians turned to 'small' magic – the close-up magician was born.

zzz

z z z

If you want to learn more about magic, find new tricks or meet other young magicians here are some of the places you could try.

www.dominicwood.co.uk

The Young Magician's Club
Centre for The Magic Arts
12 Stephenson Way
London NW1 2HD
Or visit their web site at:
www.youngmagiciansclub.co.uk

International Magic
89 Clerkenwell Road
London EC1R 5BX
Tel: 020 7405 7324

Mark Leveridge Magic
13A Lyndhurst Road
Exeter
Devon
EX2 4PA
Tel: 01392 252000
Or check out their web site:
www.markleveridge.co.uk

Davenports Magic
7 Charing Cross
Underground Shopping Arcade
The Strand
London WC2N 4HZ
Tel: 020 7836 0408

When you perform your magic you are continuing a proud tradition of magicians who have come before you. Enjoy these tricks and respect their secrets and who knows, you too could be sitting alongside the greats in the magicians' hall of fame!

MORE MAGIC

More amazing magic tricks from the fantastic Dominic Wood! If you liked learning the tricks in this book then you'll love *Dominic Wood's Spooky Magic* and *Simply Magic*.

Creepy crawlies, monsters and ghosts – find them all in this collection of creepy conjuring. Amaze your friends with vanishing eyeballs, angry genies and a dead man's finger... Plus learn how to dress up as a mummy and distract your audience for a spookily spotless spectacle!

£9.99 hardback 0 370 32766 7
The Bodley Head

With the wave of a wand and a few magic words, you will learn how to turn water into ice, or paper into money! Plus there are top tips on technique, setting the stage and looking the part to make sure you put on the perfect magic show!

£5.99 paperback 0 09 941396 5 Red Fox